# NEW SELECTED POEMS

TOM PAULIN

# New Selected Poems

FABER & FABER

First published in 2014
by Faber & Faber Ltd
Bloomsbury House
74–77 Great Russell Street
London WC1B 3DA

Typeset by RefineCatch Ltd, Bungay, Suffolk
Printed in England by Martins the Printers, Berwick upon Tweed

A CIP record for this book
is available from the British Library

ISBN 978-0-571-30798-2

2 4 6 8 10 9 7 5 3 1

# Contents

NEW SELECTED POEMS

*from* A STATE OF JUSTICE

# States

That stretch of water, it's always
There for you to cross over
To the other shore, observing
The lights of cities on blackness.

Your army jacket at the rail
Leaks its kapok into a wind
That slices gulls over a dark zero
Waste a cormorant skims through.

Any state, built on such a nature,
Is a metal convenience, its paint
Cheapened by the price of lives
Spent in a public service.

The men who peer out for dawning
Gantries below a basalt beak,
Think their vigils will make something
Clearer, as the cities close

With each other, their security
Threatened but bodied in steel
Polities that clock us safely
Over this dark; freighting us.

# Settlers

They cross from Glasgow to a black city
   Of gantries, mills and steeples. They begin to belong.
He manages the Iceworks, is an elder of the Kirk;
   She becomes, briefly, a cook in Carson's Army.
Some mornings, walking through the company gate,
   He touches the bonnet of a brown lorry.
It is warm. The men watch and say nothing.
   'Queer, how it runs off in the night,'
He says to McCullough, then climbs to his office.
   He stores a warm knowledge on his palm.

   Nightlandings on the Antrim coast, the movement of guns
Now snug in their oiled paper below the floors
   Of sundry kirks and tabernacles in that county.

# From

You've made a table you say, and are happy.
It's easy to understand where you are.
I can see you in a room we both know,
Cutting fresh wood, looking up now and then
To a window autumn light comes through.
There is a green glass float on the sill
And two stone jars we found washed by storms
On the strand. In the blueness outside, frost
And a light that, touching, makes what you see.
In that still light and silence the long hills
That ring the bay are brittle, fixed in glaze.
The island below you is a lost place
That no one can cross to in the neap,
The winter season. The tides slack,
But they never pull back; the graveyard
And ruined chapel are not to be reached now.
A priest lived there in the house when processions
Used to cross the sands slowly, in black.
Rotting boards nailed to its windows, that hermitage
Is obsolete. The light stays at that end
Of the island, catches that small, broken settlement
Where thin stones, laid flat on a humped ground,
Are carved with turnip skulls and crude bones.
A soft grass covers them and light falls.

# Inishkeel Parish Church

Standing at the gate before the service started,
In their Sunday suits, the Barrets talked together,
Smiled shyly at the visitors who packed the church
In summer. A passing congregation
Who mostly knew each other, were sometimes fashionable,
Their sons at prep school, the daughters boarding.
Inside it was as neat and tight as a boat.
Stone flags and whitewashed wails, a little brass.
Old Mrs Flewitt played the organ and Mr Alwell
Read the lessons in an accent as sharp as salt.

O Absalom, Absalom, my son,
An hour is too long, there are too many people,
Too many heads and eyes and thoughts that clutter.

Only one moment counted with the lessons
And that was when, the pressure just too much,
You walked slowly out of that packed church
Into bright cold air.
Then, before the recognitions and the talk,
There was an enormous sight of the sea,
A silent water beyond society.

# Cadaver Politic

The grey hills of that country fall away
    Like folds of skin. There are some mountains somewhere
And public parks with metal fountains.
    Rains fall and then fogs freeze, drifting
Over empty stretches of water, forts
    With broken walls on small islands.
Rafted cities smoke in the rain and sharp posts
    Have been knocked deep into flabby ground,
Thin tatters of chicken wire strung to them.
    Coffins are moored in its bays and harbours.
A damp rag, it flies several flags –
    Bunting and boneyard streamers, the badges
Of territory. In the waste, silent valleys
    Clans are at their manœuvres.
At the bottom of a cliff, on a tussock
    Of ground by a lean-to shed, a group
Of men and women huddle, watching a man
    Who tries, with damp matches, to light a board
Washed on that coast by the grey sea.

# In a Northern Landscape

Ingela is thin and she never smiles,
The man is tall and wears the same subdued colours.
Their accents might be anywhere, both seem perfect
And spend only the winter months here.
They own a stone cottage at the end of a field
That slopes to rocks and a gunmetal sea.

Their silence is part of the silence at this season,
Is so wide that these solitaries seem hemmed in
By a distance of empty sea, a bleak mewing
Of gulls perched on their chimney, expecting storm.
They sit in basket chairs on their veranda,
Reading and hearing music from a tiny transistor.

Their isolation is almost visible:
Blue light on snow or sour milk in a cheese-cloth
Resembles their mysterious element.
They pickle herrings he catches, eat sauerkraut
And make love on cold concrete in the afternoons;
Eaters of yoghurt, they enjoy austere pleasures.

At night oil lamps burn in their small windows
And blocks of pressed peat glow in a simple fireplace.
Arc lamps on the new refinery at the point
Answer their lights; there is blackness and the sound of surf.
They are so alike that they have no need to speak,
Like oppressed orphans who have won a fierce privacy.

# Under a Roof

It'll piss all evening now. From next door
The usual man and woman stuff rants on, then fades;
And I know she'll soon be moaning, climbing her little
    register
Of ecstasy till quiet settles back like dust,
Like rain, among shadows without furniture.

There was a mattress on bare floorboards when I came,
But now I own a bed, a table, and a chair
In a house where no one knows each other's name,
A zone where gardens overgrow and privet rankles –
It stinks in summer and it blinds the panes.

Cats wail at night among the weeds and bricks,
Prowl rusted fire-escapes that lose themselves
In hedges turned to scrub. Exile in the sticks
Is where I've ended up, under wet slates
Where gas flames dry the air and the meter clicks.

The girl I had scared easily. She saw
The dead bareness of the floor, her body near
Both it and mine, so dressed and left the raw,
Rough room I'd brought her to. Up here I'm free
And know a type of power, a certain kind of law.

Noises, the smell of meals, the sounds that bodies make,
All reach me here, drifting from other rooms.
And what I *know* is how much longer it will take
For thoughts and love to change themselves from these
Than rain and rooms to find their senseless lake.

# Ballywaire

My loathsome uncle chews his rasher,
My aunt is mother, pouring tea,
And this is where I live: a town
On the wrong side of the border.

A town the mountain simplifies
To spires and roofs, a bridge that spans
The river – distance shines it – and joins
Packed rural terraces. They're workless,
Costive as the smell of groceries.

Through gunfire, night arrests and searches –
The crossroads loony smashed to bits –
I keep myself intact. My body purifies.
I'll never use it.

The air greys and lights come on
In curtained parlours, our clock ticks
By last year's calendar. The quiet.
An oleograph of Pity in each kitchen.
My heart is stone. I will not budge.

# Free Colour

Evenings after rain; tenants of the rooms
Chew rinsed lettuce and watch the street.
Leading his thin mongrel by a scarf
The thin tramp stares back at a girl
Who is walking, in yellow clogs, towards town.

A grey van slurs to a stop, the bell rings
And Miss Roper watches another antique
Being carried off by the dealer.
Greener than salad, wet new leaves
Sway against the black trunks of the trees;
She wraps her cardigan and hurries in.

The van, sliding in washed light from the kerb,
Overtakes the girl who is marching
Through a green dampness in yellow clogs.

# Responsibilities

No way now, there's no way.
Geometry and rose-beds,
The light changing on the hill
Where two gravediggers glance up.
Her tears fell into your silence.

The air starved when the earth pushed.
Something made a fuck of things;
Straight and bare is all it is.
No. I kept you off, my brother,
And I'll never see your face.

# Arthur

Everyone's got someone who gave them oranges,
Sovereigns or rubbed florins,
Who wore bottle-green blazers, smoked
A churchwarden pipe on St Swithin's day,
And mulled their ale by dousing red-hot pokers
In quart jars.
But you, you're different.
You pushed off before the millions wrapped their puttees on
And ran away to sea, the prairies, New York
Where they threw you in jail when you told someone
Your blond hair made you a German spy.
After the telegram demanding
Your birth certificate
No one on the Island knew anything about you
Until the Armistice brought a letter
From a wife they'd never heard of.
You'd left her with the baby.
She wanted money.
You were somewhere in South America
In the greatest freedom, the freedom
Of nothing-was-ever-heard-of-him-since.

So I see you sometimes
Paddling up the Orinoco or the River Plate
With rifle, trusty mongrel and native mistress,
Passing cities of abandoned stucco
Draped with lianas and anacondas,
Passing their derelict opera houses
Where Caruso used to warble
Among a million bottles of imported bubbly.

Or else I watch you among the packing-case republics,
Drinking rum at the seafront in Buenos Aires
And waiting for your luck to change;
The warm sticky nights, the news from Europe,
Then the war criminals settling like bats
In the greasy darkness.

Your sister thought she saw your face once
In a crowd scene –
She went to the cinema for a week, watching
For your pale moment. She thinks
You're still alive, sitting back
On the veranda of your hacienda,
My lost great uncle, the blond
Indestructible dare-devil
Who was always playing truant and jumping
Off the harbour wall.

What I want to know is
How you did it.
How you threw off an inherited caution
Or just never knew it.
I think your grave is lost
In the mush of a tropical continent.
You are a memory that blipped out.
And though they named you from the king
Who's supposed to wake and come back
Some day,
I know that if you turned up on my doorstep,

An old sea dog with a worn leather belt
And a face I'd seen somewhere before,
You'd get no welcome.
I'd want you away.

# Firelight

Framed among ornaments, one by one
you've started to become
the faces of dead people – those
who died young, who made nothing
happen outside us, and the old
seated in armchairs like thrones,
prepared to die, but smiling.

It closes in, like the evenings
silting the tall windows.
Your voices brimmed here, but now,
dead ones, I visit you with those
glances we know. Ask me how
we got to this firelight and I'll sing
in your voices, softly, of absences.

# Bradley the Last Idealist

For some reason he never actually taught
Anyone; said a nervous complication
Prevented him, which was why his scout brought
Him over to Savoy each long vacation.
There, every morning on his own, he caught
A cable-car up into the mountains
Where he convalesced on beds of gentians.

Surrounded by blue sky and clouds, he lay
Intently staring into the far distance,
His rapt mind transfixed on Mont Blanc all day
Until absolutely locked in a deep white trance.
He left everything behind him then – the clay,
The cats, books, gowns, nodding domes and misty spires,
Those vulgar details and those Cretan liars.

At nights in term, obscured from gentlemen and God,
He clipped a torch to his air-gun, put his hat
On and prowled stealthily around the dark quad
For cats, his aim utterly accurate –
An absolute guaranteed by torch and tripod.
Then, relishing those brief feline terrors,
He would squeeze gently into their green mirrors.

# Monumental Mason

Working beside a cemetery,
Chiselling dates and names
On cheap slabs of marble
In the lighted shop window,
His meek power makes us nervous.

With his back to the street,
He cuts them in, these loves
The dead can't care about.
In his washed-out overalls
He is less a person

Than a function. People
Have grown used to him
As he sits intently
Gilding the incised letters,
A mason, displayed.

*Doris, Beloved Wife*
*And Mother,* or *Agnes*
*RIP,* their names are
Public, but we forget them,
Glimpsing a tenderness

On bald stone, some dead letters;
Or, when the traffic lulls,
Hearing from next door
The undertaker's tap, tap,
Answer his vigilant chinking.

*from* THE STRANGE MUSEUM

# Before History

Mornings when I wake too early.
There is a dead light in the room.
Rain is falling through the darkness
And the yellow lamps of the city
Are flared smudges on the wet roads.
Everyone is sleeping. I envy them.
I lie in a curtained room.
The city is nowhere then.
Somewhere, in a dank *mitteleuropa,*
I have gone to ground in a hidden street.

This is the long lulled pause
Before history happens,
When the spirit hungers for form,
Knowing that love is as distant
As the guarded capital, knowing
That the tyranny of memories
And factual establishments
Has stretched to its breaking.

# Surveillances

In the winter dusk
You see the prison camp
With its blank watchtowers;
It is as inevitable
As the movement of equipment
Or the car that carries you
Towards a violent district.

In the violet light
You watch a helicopter
Circling above the packed houses,
A long beam of light
Probing streets and waste ground.
All this might be happening
Underwater.

And if you would swop its functions
For a culture of bungalows
And light verse,
You know this is one
Of the places you belong in,
And that its public uniform
Has claimed your service.

# Traces

They are so light,
Those airmail letters.
Their blueness has fallen
From an Indian sky,
The hot taut atmosphere
Above the muddled village
Your parents write from.

'With God's help,
The crops have been brought
Safely in. All here
Are well, ten *lakhs* of rupees
Our lands are worth now.
That boy's father has twenty acres.
The buffalo are fine,
Though the heat is hard to bear.'

All the fierce passions
Of family and property
Are dictated to a scribe
Who understands English,
Has a daughter to marry
And a dusty handful
Of aluminium coins.

# Hidden Face

Her evenings are silk, a gentleness;
but the hot afternoons when her mother
bargains in the dusty market
for those two red saris that mean
she'll be married soon,
dry away her belief
in the boy she'll belong to.

The women crouch by the fire.
The sweet bitterness of the smoke blinds them
and each chappatti burns their fingers.
The pump clanks
and draws a pure water from the tubewell –
now the men bath
like patriarchs in the wide tank.
She serves them yoghurt in brass dishes.

When lights come on in the village
and a servant pads across the courtyard
to close the gates,
she walks softly on the flat roof
and gazes into a warm darkness
that might hide a face she's never seen.

If she could only walk out to meet him,
This lover who shares her sadness.

# In the Meat-Safe

There is a functional greyness
where the banal, but unusual,
has found a graceless permanence
that only the odd can admire.
Those collectors of cigarette cards
and worthless believe-it-or-not facts,
are the antiquarians of corroded
appliances who worship a dullness
as lonely as the fattest man in the world.

Solemn gaberdines, they cherish
the sweat of broken wirelesses,
goose-pimples on zinc canisters,
pre-war electric razors, sticks
of worn shaving soap, bakelite
gadgets, enemas, ration cards,
contraceptive coils that once fed
safe passions in colourless rooms
chilled by utility furniture.

Most of all they delight in
the stubble that grows on dead chins.
Recording their drab histories
in back issues of *Exchange & Mart,*
they swop this confidence – that,
in the cheap hell of starlets' accents
twittering in faded movies,
someone will sing of tinned kippers
and an ultimate boredom.

# Pot Burial

He has married again. His wife
Buys ornaments and places them
On the dark sideboard. Year by year
Her vases and small jugs crowd out
The smiles of the wife who died.

# In the Lost Province

As it comes back, brick by smoky brick,
I say to myself – strange I lived there
And walked those streets. It is the Ormeau Road
On a summer's evening, a haze of absence
Over the caked city, that slumped smell
From the blackened gasworks. Ah, those brick canyons
Where Brookeborough unsheathes a sabre,
Shouting 'No Surrender' from the back of a lorry.

And the sky is a dry purple, and men
Are talking politics in a back room.
Is it too early or too late for change?
Certainly the province is most peaceful.
Who would dream of necessity, the angers
Of Leviathan, or the years of judgement?

# Line on the Grass

Shadow in the mind,
this is its territory:
a sweep of broken ground
between two guarded towns.

A tank engine rusting
in the long grass, a man
with a fly rod wading
in the grey river.

This looks so fixed, it could
be anytime; but, scanned
in the daylight, the fields
of crops, their hawthorn hedges,

seem too visible. The men
riding black bikes stiffly
along the road are passing
a burnt-out customs post

on an asphalt apron.
They are observed passing,
passing, in a dull light:
civilians at four o'clock.

# In the Egyptian Gardens

A white mansion among cypress trees,
You will find histories inside it.
Bronze pins and sheaves of flax,
The dry shadows of a culture.

How many bibles make a Sabbath?
How many girls have disappeared
Down musky avenues of leaves?
It's an autocracy, the past.
Somewhere costive and unchanging.

I love it, but I had to leave.
The rain is falling even now,
And hell is very like those Sunday streets
Where ministers and councillors
Climb out of graves and curse at me.

# Anastasia McLaughlin

Her father is sick. He dozes most afternoons.
The nurse makes tea then and scans *The Newsletter*.
She has little to say to his grey daughter
Whose name began a strangeness the years took over.
His trade was flax and yarns, he brought her name
With an ikon and *matrioshka* – gifts for his wife
Who died the year that Carson's statue was unveiled.

McLaughlin is dreaming of a sermon he once heard
From a righteous preacher in a wooden pulpit
Who frowned upon a sinful brotherhood and shouted
The Word of deserts and rainy places where the Just
Are stretched to do the work a hard God sent them for.
His text was taken from the land of Uz
Where men are upright and their farms are walled.

'Though we may make sand to melt in a furnace
And make a mirror of it, we are as shadows
Thrown by a weaver's shuttle: and though we hide ourselves
In desolate cities and in empty houses,
His anger will seek us out till we shall hear
The accent of the destroyer, the sly champing
Of moths busy with the linen in our chests.'

He wakes to a dull afternoon like any other –
The musty dampness of his study, the window panes
That flaw his view of the lawn and settled trees.
The logs in the grate have turned to a soft ash.
The dour gardener who cut them is smoking
In the warm greenhouse, wondering did his nephew
Break in the week before and thieve McLaughlin's silver?

Constables came to the Mill House with alsatians,
And the wet spring was filled with uniforms and statements.
When they found nothing, they suspected everyone.
Even the plain woman who served them tea.
'Father, I am the lost daughter whose name you stole.
Your visions slide across these walls: dry lavender,
Old memories of all that wronged us. I am unkind.'

He sees his son below the bruised Atlantic,
And on a summer's morning in Great Victoria Street
He talks with Thomas Ferguson outside the Iceworks.
He sees the north stretched out upon the mountains,
Its dream of fair weather rubbing a bloom on rinsed slates;
He watches the mills prosper and grow derelict,
As he starts his journey to the Finland Station.

# Trotsky in Finland

*an incident from his memoirs*

The pension is very quiet. It is called
Rauha, meaning 'peace' in Finnish.
The air is transparent, perfecting
The pine trees and lakes.
He finds himself admiring the stillness
Of a pure landscape. He consumes it.
A bourgeois moment. It might be somewhere Swiss,
The wooden cuckoos calling to an uneventful
Absence, their polyglot puns
Melting in Trieste or Zürich.

The last days of autumn. The Swedish writer
Adds another sonnet to his cycle.
His English mistress drifts through the garden.
An actress, she admires her face
Bloomed in the smooth lake.
At night her giggles and frills dismay
The strictness of minor art.

They leave without paying their bill.

The owner chases them to Helsingfors.
His invisible wife is lying in the room
Above – they must give her champagne
To keep her heart beating, but she dies
While her husband screams for his money.
The head-waiter sets out to find him.
Leaving a crate of gilded bottles
By the corpse upstairs.
                              The silence here.

A thick snow is falling, the house
Is a dead monument. Insanely traditional.
He is completely alone. At nightfall
The postman carries a storm in his satchel:
The St Petersburg papers, the strike is spreading.
He asks the thin boy for his bill.
He calls for horses. Thinking,
'If this were a fiction, it would be Byron
Riding out of the Tivoli Gardens, his rank
And name set aside. Forced by more than himself.'

He crosses the frontier and speaks
To a massed force at the Institute,

Plunging from stillness into history.

# Where Art is a Midwife

In the third decade of March,
A Tuesday in the town of Z—

The censors are on day-release.
They must learn about literature.

There are things called ironies,
Also symbols, which carry meaning.

The types of ambiguity
Are as numerous as the enemies

Of the state. Formal and bourgeois,
Sonnets sing of the old order,

Its lost gardens where white ladies
Are served wine in the subtle shade.

This poem about a bear
Is not a poem about a bear.

It might be termed a satire
On a loyal friend. Do I need

To spell it out? Is it possible
That none of you can understand?

# The Strange Museum

First I woke in an upstairs drawing-room.
The curtains had been pulled back, but the house
was empty. It was furnished and oddly
quiet. A patriarch's monument.
I could see others like it in a kind of park.
Someone had built them long before in a crazed
Scottish-baronial style, foolish with turrets.
Snow had fallen during the night, so I woke
to a white silence. You had gone away.

Was this the estate of some dead, linen
millionaire? And was I some servile spirit
who knew his place in the big house and was locked
in a fierce doctrine of justification?
Somewhere among the firs and beeches, there was
a god of curses who wished us both dead.
His finger was on the trigger. He was insane.
The vindictive shadow, I thought, he scatters
bodies everywhere and has broken the city.

I blamed him then, for I too had been touched;
my notion of freedom was like the curved chairs
in that room. A type of formal elegance.
Had you been there we would have made love
in that strange museum, but it would still
have oppressed us with its fixed anger.
I knew then, in that chill morning, that this
was the house I had lived in once, that I was through
with the polite dust of bibles, the righteous pulpits.

So, later, I woke in a tennis suburb.
History could happen elsewhere, I was free now
in a neat tame place whose gods were milder.
A cold dawn, but a different season.
There was the rickety fizz of starlings
trying to sing, and a grey tenderness.
I was happy then, knowing the days had changed
and that you would come back here, to this room.
You were the season, beyond winter, the first freshness.

# A Lyric Afterwards

There was a taut dryness all that summer
and you sat each day in the hot garden
until those uniformed comedians
filled the street with their big white ambulance,
fetching you and bringing you back to me.

Far from the sea of ourselves we waited
and prayed for the tight blue silence to give.
In your absence I climbed to a square room
where there were dried flowers, folders of sonnets
and crossword puzzles: call them musical

snuffboxes or mannered anachronisms,
they were all too uselessly intricate,
caskets of the dead spirit. Their bitter
constraints and formal pleasures were a style
of being perfect in despair; they spoke

with the vicious trapped crying of a wren.
But that is changed now, and when I see you
walking by the river, a step from me,
there is this great kindness everywhere:
now in the grace of the world and always.

*from* LIBERTY TREE

# Under Creon

Rhododendrons growing wild below a mountain
and no long high wall or trees either;
a humped road, bone-dry, with no one –
passing one lough and then another
where water-lilies glazed, primed like traps.

A neapish hour, I searched out gaps
in that imperial shrub: a free voice sang
dissenting green, and syllables spoke
holm oaks by a salt shore, their dark tangs
glistening like Nisus in a night attack.

The daylight gods were never in this place
and I had pressed beyond my usual dusk
to find a cadence for the dead: McCracken,
Hope, the northern starlight, a death mask
and the levelled grave that Biggar traced;

like an epic arming in an olive grove
this was a stringent grief and a form of love.
Maybe one day I'll get the hang of it
and find joy, not justice, in a snapped connection,
that Jacobin oath on the black mountain.

# Desertmartin

At noon, in the dead centre of a faith,
Between Draperstown and Magherafelt,
This bitter village shows the flag
In a baked absolute September light.
Here the Word has withered to a few
Parched certainties, and the charred stubble
Tightens like a black belt, a crop of Bibles.

Because this is the territory of the Law
I drive across it with a powerless knowledge –
The owl of Minerva in a hired car.
A Jock squaddy glances down the street
And grins, happy and expendable,
Like a brass cartridge. He is a useful thing,
Almost at home, and yet not quite, not quite.

It's a limed nest, this place. I see a plain
Presbyterian grace sour, then harden,
As a free strenuous spirit changes
To a servile defiance that whines and shrieks
For the bondage of the letter: it shouts
For the Big Man to lead his wee people
To a clean white prison, their scorched tomorrow.

Masculine Islam, the rule of the Just,
Egyptian sand dunes and geometry,
A theology of rifle-butts and executions:
These are the places where the spirit dies.
And now, in Desertmartin's sandy light,
I see a culture of twigs and bird-shit
Waving a gaudy flag it loves and curses.

# 'What Kind of Formation are B Specials?'

The franked letter
lay on the chill tiles
like a writ:
I bent to lift it and saw
this different mark –
magenta and military –
across one corner,
then split the edge and read,
*Warszawa, 9/12/81.*
Yards off, a train leant
on ice and metal,
and I was a zero
in a safe house
asking who was it
crossed the packed snow
with this misdirected, late,
uncandid message
to Anglia, their Anglia?
That fremd evening
I tried to connect
the signs under my eyes
with the state official
who'd scanned your lines,
for now that I've learnt
the oppressor's alphabet
I live in the half-light
of a strange
shivering translation
where the kingdom of letters
is like the postal system

of a frozen state
and your last question
slips through like code.
Now I go down
among the glubbed carp
of catholic Europe
that taste of mud and penance
this Christmas Eve,
and in the belly
of a non-nation
admire a chosen hunger . . .
but I still can't pray,
end, or send this letter.

# Off the Back of a Lorry

A zippo lighter
and a quilted jacket,
two rednecks troughing
in a gleamy diner,
the flinty chipmarks
on a white enamel pail,
Paisley putting pen to paper
in Crumlin jail,
a jumbo double
fried peanut butter
sandwich Elvis scoffed
during the last
diapered days –
they're more than tacky,
these pured fictions,
and like the small ads
in a country paper
they build a gritty
sort of prod baroque
I must return to
like my own boke.

## Argument from Design

Your glooby voice
is salt and carrageen,
a dolphin fountain
among the bay trees
in a Tuscan garden
where a dwarf on a tortoise
guards the pearly grotto;
and your quaint frizz
has this ebony wrinkle
glazed with bruised purple,
an aubergine lip,
a barbel-beard.
What a baroque smörgåsbord!
bad taste of the blond north
doing a flip
with the sugars of the deep south.

# A Rum Cove, a Stout Cove

On the Barrack Islands far out
in the South Atlantic
the great-great-grandson (Sol Grout)
of Nelson's last bosun
is packing crawfish into a thick
barnacled keepbox marked *Briton
Kanning Factors Illimitated.*
It's his swart locks and cochin cheeks
that glim in the top left-hand corner
of 'Bold Bessie', the prime banner
that longs to LOL 301.
Like Gib, like the god called M'Lud,
and those tars behind locked doors
whistling *Britannia Rules*
in their slow skrimshandering
with worn and corded tools,
he's firm, Sol Grout, to the core,
the genius of these used islands
where no maritime elegists sing
of Resolution or Independence
with their harbourmaster's stores,
clagged mountains of ashy shale
and a small bird that no one has named –
a flightless timorous landrail
whose cry is rusted, hard, like chains.

# Black Bread

*for Ann Pasternak Slater*


Splitting birches, spiky thicket, kinship –
this is the passionate, the phonic surface
I can take only on trust, like a character
translated to a short story whose huge language
he doesn't know. So we break black bread
in the provinces and can't be certain
what it is we're missing, or what sacrament
this might be, the loaf wrapped in a shirt-tail
like a prisoner's secret or a caked ikon,
that is sour and good, and has crossed over versts,
kilometres, miles. It's those journeys
tholed under the salt stars, in the eager wind
that starves sentries and students in their long coats.
Claudius is on the phone, hear that hard
accent scraping its boots on the threshold,
his thick acid voice in your uncle's conscience,
*I'd have known better how to defend my friend.*
Bitter! Bitter! Bitter! the wedding-guests chant
in bast sandals, the pickled cucumbers
cry out in a prickly opera and round grains
of coriander stud the desert crust.
It's a lump of northern peat, itself alone,
and kin to the black earth, to shaggy speech;
I'll taste it on my tongue next year in the holy,
freed city of gold and parchment.

# A Written Answer

This poem by Rupert Brookeborough
is all about fishing and the stout B-men
(they live for always in our hearts,
their only crime was being loyal),
there is a lough in it and stacks of rivers,
also a brave wee hymn to the sten-gun.
The poet describes Gough of the Curragh
and by his use of many metric arts
he designs a fictionary universe
which has its own laws and isn't quite
the same as this place that we call real.
His use of metonymy is pretty desperate
and the green symbolism's a contradiction,
but I like his image of the elm and chestnut,
for to me this author is a fly man
and the critics yonder say his work is alright.

# Manichean Geography II

Banal hours in muggy weather.
The slack wind – warm, trammelled –
Is named for a freighter
That dumped its clotted chains
In Prince Darling Bay.
*One time, sometime, never again old chug.*

From a rainwood pulpit
The Reverend Spanner McTavish
Preaches a burnt sermon
On the injustice of the Copra Board
While an Anglican head-hunter
Reads *Phrenology Made Easy*
And fidgets with his namba.
*One time, sometime, never again old chug.*

Sunset and a frigate-bird
Circling the chalk lighthouse.
In a twilight of flying foxes
The coconut crabs are shredding
O-level papers in English Literature,
As a pidgin ode is chanted
In the deepy rainforest
To a signed photograph
Of his High Troppo Majesty
The Duke of Edinburgh.
*One time, sometime, never again old chug.*
To bossy saltmen from wayback
The islands are a spatched necklace
Of prickly heat, boils,

And choggy boredom.
Big Ben Man, where is?
Asks the girl whose white teeth
Have the blank snowy dazzle
Of coconut flesh.
Just look what we've made
Of your damned islands, we answer.
They are images now
– Never again old chug –
Images of our own disgust.

# A Nation, Yet Again

*after Pushkin*

That kitsch lumber-room is stacked
with a parnassian dialect:
'love, hope, and quiet reputation
kissed us for a short season
and the gamey letters that we swopped,
in clipped verse, soon had to stop.'
No one, then, praised either side,
though some dipped down among the shades
to find Aeneas and to file
a delicate, a tough, new style
that draws the language to the light
and purifies its tribal rites.
I'm tense now: talk of sharing power,
prophecies of civil war,
new reasons for a secular
mode of voicing the word *nation*
set us on edge, this generation,
and force the poet to play traitor
or act the half-sure legislator.
No matter; there's a classic form
that's in the blood, that makes me warm
to better, raise, build up, refine
whatever gabbles without discipline:
see, it takes me now, these hands stir
to bind the northern to the southern stars.

# Local Histories

A khaki bell-tent in the mopane forest:
Professor 'Deeko' Kerr is on vacation
Observing the delicate birds of Africa.
He leaves his russet hide to take a leak,
'What I have, I hold,' he thinks as the boy
Sneaks a quick gander at his pinko prong.
Chit-chat evaporates at this charred altitude
Like letters airmailed to Great Namaland
Or Deeko's postcards to his old headmaster
Who wrote the school would be most pleased to learn
Of his promotion to the Chair of Social Justice
At Jan Smuts College in the Orange Free State.
He thanked him also for his learned article,
'Samuel Twaddell: a Co. Down Man at the Cape'.
Even now, at a bring-and-buy in Cleaver Park,
His Aunt Mina is telling Lady Lowry,
'That boy's gone far, but we've heard nothing yet.'

# A Daily Beauty

*Before he emigrated to Philadelphia, John Dunlap,*
*the printer of the Declaration of Independence, was an*
*apprentice in Gray's printing-shop in Main Street.*

A tray of waspy plums and American apples,
three yards of cracked oilcloth tacked to the counter,
that mild pong of ham, pan loaves, the paraffin tang
of newsprint from a stack of sisalled papers:
the *Derry Journal, Weekly News,* and *Strabane Chronicle.*
It's buzzy slapdash in and out: a private's squatting
on an elsan in the sangar by the humpy bridge,
as *Bannigan's Gravels* rakes through its gear-box
and the auctioneer's voice drills the clabbery market
like a scorching lark over a prison yard.
There's Union Street and Barrack Street, and here's me
just an ignoramus with a jammy piece,
taking a holyer in these slurried townlands.

# Of Difference Does it Make

*During the 51-year existence of the Northern Ireland
Parliament only one Bill sponsored by a non-Unionist
member was ever passed.*

Among the plovers and the stonechats
protected by the Wild Birds Act
of nineteen-hundred-and-thirty-one,
there is a rare stint called the notawhit
that has a schisty flight-call, like the chough's.
*Notawhit, notawhit, notawhit*
– it raps out a sharp code-sign
like a mild and patient prisoner
pecking through granite with a teaspoon.

# From the Death Cell: Iambes VIII

*after Chénier*

We live: – dishonoured, in the shit. So what? it had to be.
  This is the pits and yet we feed and sleep.
Even here – penned in, watered and waiting for the chop
    (just place your bets) – affairs take off,
there's gossip, bitching and a pecking-order.
  Songs, jokes, card-schools; she lifts her skirts; someone
bops a tight balloon against the window-panes.
  It's like the speeches of those seven hundred eejits
(Barrère's the shiftiest of the lot) – a comic fart
    we whoop and cheer and then forget.
One jumps, another skips; that greasy pack
    of gut and gullet politicians raps and hoots
until, dead quick, the door scrakes open
    and our tiger-masters' wee pimp struts in.
Who's getting it today? We freeze and listen,
    then all but one of us knows it isn't him . . . .

# Foot Patrol, Fermanagh

A pierrepoint stretch, mid-afternoon;
the last two go facing back
down the walled street below the chestnuts
this still claggy Sabbath.
They hold their rifles lightly, like dipped rods,
and in a blurt of sunshine
the aluminium paint on the customs shed
has a dead shine like a text
brushed onto basalt.
It's not that anything will happen next
in this hour that is as constant
as sin, and as original,
though why is it they remind me
of a prisoner led singing down a corridor
to a floor that isn't a floor any longer?

*from* The Book of Juniper

In the original liturgy
on a bare island

a voice seeks an answer
in the sea wind:

'The tides parted and I crossed
barefoot to Inishkeel.

Where was the lost crozier
among the scorched bracken?

And where was that freshet
of sweet water?

Goose-grass and broken walls
were all my sanctuary,

I mistook a drowsed hour
for the spirit's joy;

on a thymy headland
I entered

the strict soul
of a dry cricket.

Heat haze and wild flowers,
a warm chirring all

that civil afternoon,
till its classic song

failed me and I sighed
for a different love

in grey weather.'

\*

Tougher than the wind
it keeps a low profile
on rough ground.
Rugged, fecund,
with resined spines,
the gymnosperm
hugs the hillside
and wills its own survival.
The subtle arts are still to happen
and in the eye of a needle
a singing voice
tells a miniature epic
of the boreal forest:
not a silk tapestry
of fierce folk
warring on the tundra
or making exquisite love
on a starry counterpane,
but an in-the-beginning
was a wintry light
and *juniperus*.

*

Though it might be a simple
decoration
or a chill fragrance
in a snug souterrain,
I must grasp again
how its green
springy resistance
ducks its head down and skirts
the warped polities of other trees
bent in the Atlantic wind.
For no one knows
if nature allowed it
to grow tall
what proud grace
the juniper tree might show
that flared, once, like fire
along the hills.

*

On this coast
it is the only
tree of freedom
to be found,
and I imagine
that a swelling army is marching
from Memory Harbour and Killala
carrying branches
of green juniper.

Consider
the gothic zigzags
and brisk formations
that square to meet
the green tide rising
through Mayo and Antrim,

now dream
of that sweet
equal republic
where the juniper
talks to the oak,
the thistle,
the bandaged elm,
and the jolly jolly chestnut.

*from* FIVEMILETOWN

# The Bungalow on the Unapproved Road

The mattress on their bed
was so spongy
we fell all night
into a cut-price nothing
that wrecked our backs.
The headboard was padded
with black vinyl –
just the ugliest thing
I'd seen in a long time,
though the new wallpaper
they'd bought in Wellworths –
tequila sunsets
on the Costa Brava –
might take the biscuit.
That May morning
I looked out at the Bluestacks
and the Glen River –
a wet, chittering
smash of light
where a black Vauxhall
jeuked round a bend
on jammy springs,
like a patched Oldsmobile
heading for Donegal
with a raft of hooch in the trunk.

# Peacetime

We moved house
in '63.

My brother cried
quietly in his room.

Stuff in the loft,
my dad said burn it.

I cut the brass buttons
from his khaki tunic,

sploshed petrol,
felt in the back pocket

of the heavy trousers –
no wallet,

only four sheets
of folded bog-roll

(he'd been an officer
and planned ahead).

I chucked a match.
*Whap!*

# Fivemiletown

The release of putting off
who and where we've come from,
then meeting in this room
with no clothes on –
to believe in nothing,
to be nothing.

Before you could reach out
to touch my hand
I went to the end of that first
empty motorway
in a transit van
packed with gauze sacks
of onions.
I waited in groundmist
by a hedge
that was webbed with little frost nets –
pointlessly early
and on edge,
it was like rubbing one finger
along the dulled blade
of a penknife,
then snapping it shut.
I need only go back,
though all of my life
was pitched in the risk
of seeing and touching you.

A church and a creamery,
the trope of villages

on the slow road to Enniskillen
where they made a stramash
of the Imperial Hotel
two days before
our last prime minister
was whipped to Brize Norton
at smokefall.

When I found the guest-house
opposite Byrne's Hardware
the girl, Bridie, said 'Nah,
she's not back yet –
d'you want wait on her?'
But I went off
down the main street
like the place was watching
this gaberdine stranger
who'd never seen it before.

There was a newish wood
above a small, still lough
so I climbed into its
margin of larch and chestnut,
one of those buck eejits
that feels misunderstood –
the pious, dogged friend
who's brought just comfort,
no more than that.

I smoked a cigarette
while an olive armoured car

nosed down the hill –
no more than I could, it'd never fit
the manor house's *porte cochère*
and white oriel,
for I felt dwammy sick
at the fact of meeting you again
so near and far from home
and never saying
let's run from every one of them.

There was a half-hour
when I could still
slip back to The Velma
and leave a note with her –
*I called but you weren't in.*
*See you.*

# Rosetta Stone

We were real good
and got to share a desk
that smelt like the head's Bible
when I lifted up its lid
and nicked a sharp HB
from Eileen's leather pouch,
knowing that she knew
but would never tell on me.
There wasn't a single hair
between our sleeping legs
that I could ever see –
only that spiky *différance*
waiting on history.
Hers was a little plum,
mine a scaldy that could pee
yella as the tartan skirt
she slid one tiny bit
to let me touch her pumice-silk,
chalky like my glans might be.

# Voronezh

*Anna Akhmatova*


You walk on permafrost
in these streets.
The town's silly and heavy
like a glass paperweight
stuck on a desk –
a wide steel one
glib as this pavement.
I trimp on ice,
the sledges skitter and slip.
Crows are crowding the poplars,
and St Peter's of Voronezh
is an acidgreen dome
fizzing in the flecked light.
The earth's stout as a bell –
it hums like that battle
on the Field of Snipes.
Lord let each poplar
take the shape of a wine-glass
and I'll make it ring
as though the priest's wed us.
But that tin lamp
on the poet's table
was watched last night –
Judas and the Word
are stalking each other
through this scroggy town
where every line has three stresses
and only the one word, *dark*.

# Where's this Big River Come From?

We were walking back along the Lagan
me and Noel Sloan,
two schoolkids wanting to be writers.
'Could you make new words up?'
he asked me, 'not puns but.'
I said that *sdark* was the only one
had ever slipped into my head.
'It's wick, though – too Nordic don't you reckon?'
I felt a bit like a bishop saying that.
Noel kept quiet, till at Queen's Bridge
he asked, 'D'you ever say *jap*?'
We could try stick it to a spat of water.

# 'There are many wonders on this earth'

### *Chorus from* Antigone

There are many wonders on this earth
and man has made the most of them,
though only death has baffled him
he owns the universe, the stars,
*sput* satellites and great societies.

Fish pip inside his radar screens
and foals kick out of a syringe:
he bounces on the dusty moon
and chases clouds about the sky
so they can dip on sterile ground.

By pushing harder every way,
by risking everything he loves,
he makes us better, day by day:
we call this progress and it shows
we're damned near perfect!

# Breez Marine

It was my birthday
in the Europort
a Polish barber
cut my hair so short
that a young squaddy
came blinking out
– chin smooth
legs unsteady –
into that glazed street
they call Coldharbour.
We waited three minutes
by the photobooth
– some early warning –
and me and her
we fought a battle
'bout my hair
and my blue passport.
She laughed at me
by that barbarous pole
so rudely forced
and when the wet prints
slid through the hole
shrieked *just as well*
*we'll never marry*
*would y'look at those?*
Each stunned eye
it shone like a dog's nose
pointing at a prison dinner.
All I could try
was turn a sly

hurt look to soften her
and that night in bed
I stuck my winedark tongue
inside her bum
her blackhaired Irish bum
repeating in my head
his father's prayer
to shite and onions.
But my summum pulchrum
said *I've had enough*
*we rubbed each other up*
*a brave long while*
*that's never love.*

# I Am Nature

*Homage to Jackson Pollock, 1912–1956*


I might be the real
> Leroy McCoy
> landsurveyor
> way out west
> of Gila River

you know I pushed my
> soft bap
> out her funky vulva
> her black thighs
> and my first cry
> was Scotch–Irish
> a scrake
> a scratch
> a *screighulaidh*

I passed nights
> sidewinding
> on the desert floor
> fertil arid zone
> smoke trees
> creosote bush
> ironwood
> Joshua trees

till I lit
> on dreamtime
> wrote my nose
> in sand

                    the infants'
                    burying-ground

I did learn for sure there
                    smoketaste
                    piñon
                    chicken flesh
                    mesquite

and turned wise
                    as sagebrush

smart as the tabs
                    on a 6-pack
                    as cat's claw
                    chickenwire
                    thorn

I flicked fast through the switches
                    licking her oils
                    blood gunge
                    paintjuice
                    gumbo
                    Stella McClure
                    off of my skin

rubbed all of them back but
                    hear me sister!
                    brother believe me!

just banging on
>like a bee in a tin
>like the burning bush

cracking dipping and dancing
>like I'm the last
>real Hurrican Higgin
>critter and Cruthin
>scouther and skitter
>witness witness
>WITNESS TREE!

# Last Statement

*Vladimir Mayakovsky*


It's after one,
you're in the sack, I guess.
The stars are echoed
in the Volga's darkness
and I'm not fussed
or urgent anymore.
I won't be wiring you
my slogans and my kisses
in daft capitals:
we bit green chillies
and we're through.
We were like lovers
leaning from a ferry
on the White Canal –
our arguments, statistics,
our fucks and cries
notched on the calculus.
Ack, the night has jammed
each signal from the stars,
and this, this is my last
stittering, grief-splintered
call-sign to the future.
Christ, I want to wow
both history and technology . . .
I could tell it to the world right now.

# An Ulster Unionist Walks the Streets of London

All that Friday
there was no flag –
no Union Jack,
no tricolour –
on the governor's mansion.
I waited outside the gate-lodge,
waited like a dog
in my own province
till a policeman brought me
a signed paper.
Was I meant to beg
and be grateful?
I sat on the breakfast-shuttle and I called –
I called out loud –
to the three Hebrew children
for I know at this time
there is neither prince, prophet, nor leader –
there is no power
we can call our own.
I grabbed a fast black –
ack, I caught a taxi –
to Kentish Town,
then walked the streets
like a half-foreigner
among the London Irish.
What does it feel like?
I wanted ask them –
what does it feel like
to be a child of that nation?

But I went underground
to the Strangers' House –
*We vouch*, they swore,
*We deem*, they cried,
till I said, 'Out . . .
I may go out that door
and walk the streets
searching my own people.'

# From *Landsflykt*

*August Strindberg*

I heard a voice out of Europe
a southern accent
Away to hell, England,
you're so dry on the outside
dry and chalky
but your inside's like a coal barge
parked between the North Sea and the Atlantic
an island of warehouses and corner shops
– they all smell of bacon and stale bread
down with Disraeli
damn the Anglican Church
damn your pious women
who knit and make tea
damn your imperial males
all sabres and pricks
your cheapo novels your daily Godawful papers
your mission halls and Salvation Army

Then I answered out of the North
you're all beef, sin, coal, chalk
but that's no matter
don't think I'm taken in
by your lovely bottles of Pale Ale
your neat warm pubs
or your excellent razor blades
– no, I forgive you
I forgive your crimes in Africa, India, Ireland
– I'm letting you off the hook, Albion,

not for your own sake, never,
but because out of your steam presses
shot Dickens, Darwin, Spencer and Mill!

# Really Naff

He'd cropped hair
and a sweater –
a tight one on bare skin.
Something too full about the face
but shy with it.
A bit like a tope –
a tope or an airplane
if you seen them from above.
There was this warning flag
at the quarry –
someone's underpants strung on a pole
by a concrete hut.
I felt the blast stub the hill
then we climbed up a track
past Lough Free they call it.
We drove home the next day.
My eyes were wide open,
I stared down –
it's the thrash of new love –
at these scribbly lines
in the Ormeau Baths.
I notched his neck with my lips.
In bed he was all thumbs –
I was jabbed like a doorbell –
until he collapsed
sticky with the promise
of making my bum.
Which he didn't.
So I call him Mr Thumb
and draw eyes on that face

with a felt tip –
flat as a pancake
or a kid's drawing.
I put in ocean, fathoms, light,
but he's as bare as need, poor guy,
or the sole of that trainer.

# The Defenestration of Hillsborough

Here we are on a window ledge
with the idea of race.

All our victories
were defeats really

and the tea chests in that room
aren't packed with books.

The door's locked on us
so we begin again

with cack on the sill
and *The Book of Analogies.*

It falls open at a map
of the small nations of Europe,

it has a Lutheran engraving
of Woodrow Wilson's homestead

in a cloon above Strabane,
and it tells you Tomáš Masaryk

was a locksmith's apprentice.
This means we have a choice:

either to jump or get pushed.

*from* WALKING A LINE

# Klee/Clover

Nightwatch after nightwatch
Paul Klee endured
'horribly boring guard duty'
at the gasoline cellar
and every morning
outside the Zeppelin hangar
there was drill then a speech
tacked with junk formulas
he varnished wings
and stencilled numbers
next to gothic insignia
a private first-class
with a lippy dislike
of their royal majesties
and *Flying School 5 (Bavaria)*

he wrote home to Lily
*it's nice this spring weather*
*and now we've laid out a garden*
*between the second and third runways*
*the airfield's becoming*
*more and more beautiful*
each time a plane crashed
– and that happened quite often
he cut squares of canvas
from the wings and fuselage
he never said why
but every smashed biplane
looked daft or ridiculous
halfjoky and untrue

– maybe the pilots annoyed him?
those unlovely aristos
who never knew they were flying
primed blank canvases
into his beautiful airfield

# History of the Tin Tent

During the first push on the Somme
a temporary captain
in the Royal Engineers
– Peter Nissen a Canadian
designed an experimental
steel tent
that could be erected
from stacked materials
by an NCO and eight men
in 110 minutes

so the Nissen hut is the descendant
and enriched relation
of the Elephant and other
similar steel structures
that were adopted then adapted
for trench warfare

sheets of corrugated iron
beaverjoints purlins joists
wire nails and matchboard lining
were packed into kits
so complete societies
could be knocked and bent
into sudden being
by a squad of soldiers with a truck
a few tools
and a pair of ladders

barracks hospital
mess hall and hangar

– chapel shooting-range petrol dump *&c*
they were all bowed into shape
from rippling thundery
hundredweight acres
of sheet metal
Europe became a desert
so these tents could happen
though they now seem banal
like the word *forever*

all over England
on farmland and airfields
these halfsubmerged sheds
have a throwaway permanence
a never newpainted
sense of duration
that exists anywhere
and belongs nowhere
– ribbed basic
set fast in pocked concrete
they're almost like texts
no one wants to read
– texts prefabs caves
a whole aesthetic in reverse

# Matins

A tinniness in that bell
– I was ten when I heard it first
its sad but urgent tang
binging across two dead –
you could hardly call them fields
and there it goes again
off-key but beating out
its meek unsettled belief
on a shore of this small republic
not a *cloche fêlée* for sure
just Anglican Irish and poor

maybe I'll cross those acres
– deadness and brambles just
between our house and the church?
go into that half-strange porch
its odour of damp and limewash
strawbottomed chairs and slack
well loose little case of hymnals
it must be a tribal thing
this wanting to go back there
(d'you want to kneel in prayer?)
this wishing the words were firm
with a bit of a kick and a skip
why couldn't they stay the same
and sing *bing-ding bing-ding?*

# The Firhouse

There's nothing else handy
only this bit of blottingpaper
I'm trying to make notes on
with a gummy fountain pen that either dries or blurs
as if it knows this poem (if it *is* a poem)
will never quite get written
but right now I have to put down something
about this curious house off a main road
maybe a mile or so from a dormitory village near Gotham
(bit sinister that name but it's better than Bunny)
the house is set next a clump of fir trees on a small hill
and looks out over a wide flat valley
where nothing much ever happened

it has coppercoloured rooftiles
that seem like they're made of baked felt
the walls are cream snowcem
and the roof's pitched just a shade too steep
though you could say the angle of it
echoes the shape the fir trees make
– diagrammatic like the TV aerial
clamped tight to the sentrybox chimney
a roofslope cut into by the Velux window
that makes another angle when it's opened

whoever built this liked squares and triangles too much
and they were obsessed by fussy additions –
the outbuildings are a mess permanently unfinished
like furry shoeboxes stuck together
the rosebushes are packed tight the way they are in a nursery

the garden's jammed with overgrown Christmas trees
and webby fernspray cypresses
a sign at the far end says CONIFERS ⟶

isn't there something strained something perky but daft
about this bit of rural real estate this homey place of business
like a pocket telephone exchange out on its own
but warmed and protected by the fir trees?
there's a dormobile parked to one side
and hosepipe trailing across the lawn like a cable
planes land in the airport down in the valley
cropsprayers floom over huge fields of yellow rape
there's a big bendy river
and on summer days all the colours come out loud and clear
like a Festival of Britain painting
I've been sitting here for the last half-hour
in my muddy VW
watching the house from the lane
– it has a sign by the gate saying *Keeper's Cottage*
and now I feel like a man obsessed with the woman who lives
    there
a man who should be at work and either feels guilty
or looks suspicious or is somehow out of place

there she is at the kitchen window washing dishes
while I'm inventing an excuse to call
– *D'you sell conifers?* I ask when she opens the door
she's fortyish with pale skin and sisalish hair
wears a grey mohair jumper eyes blue
a speck of yellow sleepyolk in the left one

– *Conifers!* she laughs *oh we used to* –
*I keep telling my husband to take that silly sign down*
– *He's given up on the trees?*
– *We stopped them last winter there just wasn't a market*
– *I'm sorry to bother you now*
she forces a smile and shuts the door

walking back to the car it's like I'm on the edge of a secret
something to do with a closed door and the word *they*
a sort of riddle
who was it said *take it from me son*
*they never invite you in?*
but why should you want in? why should there be
some little *puja* room you have to come inside of?
only there's times you notice some slight subtle difference
in the emotional weather
a cut-off point or an absence
because really you're a stranger and who wants a stranger
in their own house?
from now on in
I'll be writing in a vacuum about a vacuum
– *there's no such thing as society*
*only men and women living together*
*on the great open site of human freedom*
so in the east midlands of England
you'll find the first and last frontier
and then face the question – could anyone write it?

# L

Tongue *lingua*
it enters small apertures
that are hairy wet waxy
or taste of old hapennies
the kind you sucked as a kid
or laid out on a railtrack
so the train to Helen's Bay
could punch them into sharp haloes

often it relishes
the faint kidney flavour
of some defunct sandstone *pissoir*
behind overgrown bushes

in undercover skirmishes
it acts as love's secret agent
a diligent sapper that digs
into ears and emery armpits
or slides between fingers and toes

it penetrates the bum on state occasions
and searches the *mons pubis*
for a fleshy button
a tiny wee *cep*
*plink plonk* it endures the juice of scallions
and longs to slither
into a left nostril

like a heifer drawn to the rocks
it loves to lick salt
and dwell on the sea's minerals

[99]

with a fur of tannin on it like a mole
and hiding a soft saggy underbelly
this tongue thing's a supple instrument
kinda decent and hardworking
and often more welcome than the penis
– too many poems speak for that member
maybe it's time I unbuttoned my tongue?

## Painting with Sawdust

This may sound insane
but if you take the way a saw
goes ripping and tearing
through a plank of pine or larch
– pine's a softwood while larch
is hard like bone
– if you listen to a saw giving out
those barking yelpy groans
those driven shouts and moans
that're wild as a drowning pup
or raw
like a wet shammy rubbing its knuckles
on a windowpane
– if you listen to the crazy chuckles
thrown out by a saw
in the heat of its only function in life
though to be strictly accurate that jagged blade
can't ever belong to what we call life
– if you reflect on the noises this knife
– this big thrawn toothy rather tinny knife
must make
then they might be a version those chuckles
of the way couples it's said
*are always going in and out*
*of intimacy*
which means that when the saw's
dogged panting
suddenly whoops screams and stops
– *chup!*
there's a change of tune

because now that its constant whuffing
has let up
one lover or the other must take a brush
not to paint a picture but lick up
what it seems such a pity not to leave behind
or leave new and untouched
– that tiny dune
of resiny sweet crumbs

## What's Natural

Taking a line out for a walk
ought to seem – well
second nature
like the way you laugh or talk
– though both speech and laughter
have to be learned
inside a culture
which means that when you take a pencil
and let the line go wandering
upon its lead
– or on its lead
there is
somewhere between a pun
and a tautology
this little yolky sun that wishes
it could just squeeze over the horizon
and chuck itself – splittery
splattery
all over the scrake
– the wheeze and piss
of dawn

# Sparrowgrass

Though it's different from goosegrass
to say it corrupts
from out *asparagus*
would be wrong
and though sparrows
don't like to be seen in long grass
*sparrowgrass* is its own concept
light and wavy like the smoky bush
that grows and grows
into a soft flumy
a feathery delicacy
when you let that strange
Greek or Roman head
drive its roots deeply
into a rich gritty bed

# Soldier and Packman

*in memory Chanda Singh Khosa, 1908–1993*

The old havildar
makes angry in the courtyard
he takes an iron bar
to the water buffalo
then stops and lets out a roar
like a trapped bull
– not a week goes by but he casts out
his eldest son
and heaps curses on his daughters
– Gurbaksh Sarbjit
Manjit Srinderjit
them be no bloody good 'tall
Tarsem – Chin-DAY!
you'm get out!
now he calls for a chota peg
chota chota peg scherab!
but what he craves is a slug
from the litre bottle of Johnny Walker
that Swaran Kaur keeps by the rifle
in the padlocked press

we watch him lying
on a stringbed by the tubewell
every so often he sighs
– from Jullundur Canton
to Shipquay Street
from the railway sidings at Simla
to Small Heath or the Bogside
he's sent out naked again

– I'm a done man Tom
soon be dead – all finish!
him be your son Binday

dear father
old sinner
the risktaker the beloved
I watch your daughters cry their eyes out
then sift the ghat in prayer
for all that's left of our pitaji
what does it mean to forgive?
would you tell me?
– first ting you must be love
then maybe you'm die like me
shantih shantih

# The Sting

Anyone who has ever been hit
straight in the eye by a wasp
knows it's a bit like being poked
by the good Lord's little finger
– it resembles that moment
when the windshield binges
into quartzy toffee
the moment when it's only too clear
– too crystal clear –
that something has broken through
the riotshield that jigs
between self and reality
– it's simply a rehearsal
for the big finger
and it's what happened me
that summer afternoon
near Strabane
though as Tosser McCrossan would say
*if thon's all't hit you man*
*then you're lucky!*
or as you might add yourself
*I'm sure a wee sting*
*'ll leave your ego still intact*
but the fact is
this boy got stung
as we walked by the River Mourne
past Sion Mills
– I was staring at the yellow factory
dozens of windows and windowsills
all summery industry

when that stupid wasp
came zizzing across the river
and ruined my little ploy
for my heart it was set
on the tiny wee hasp
that showed through your cheesecloth blouse
– neither yoghurt nor cheese my love
but sugar brown sugar brown sugar
– but we couldn't dive down in the grass
for my sudden new patch of flesh
was hardly a turn-on that day
– just imagine
there'd have reared above you
the small bare ass
of that closed that stretched eyelid
blind and bald like a scaldy
or some indignant vulture
– *wouldn't you rather go back to the house?*
but as we continued our dander
you seemed relieved
and I felt – well – shrived
it was a pilgrimage of a kind
as we left that plonky
invented village behind
pushing through shives
of chippy sunlight
and the birds' *sip sip sip*
you with your brown lovely skin
me with my carrion eye
– then across the river

happened this curtainless manse
with a collapsed stone wall
and an orchard
all lichened and neglected
except that from out it the air
suthered a ripeness of plums
across the wimpling water
I closed my good eye
– what brushed my unkissed lips
like a prayer
was the blue grapes of Gilead

# Air Plane

Foursquare
a dead duck
– but a duck's not square
only if you say it is
say it and sigh

as for me I'd like to paint
or model a square duck
– *squak! squak!* it cries
its nest a bunker
its flightpath some buried cable
its eggs like building blocks
pure cubes of planed wood
or plastic bright blue plastic

why bother with such a creature?
I'll tell you why
– because so many poems
are like square ducks
that is they contrive
to be both tame and just
tucked out of harm's way
at the bottom of a column
these verbal machines
are definite
yes very definite
even when they're sad
they want us to love
their rigid waddle
their ticktock cries

the way they confront
our square earth
in its box of –
I should say *sky*
– in its box of air

*from* THE WIND DOG

## Kingstown St Vincent

– piece of paper that's been wet then dried
it's a different texture – rougher
a bit like a voice from the other side
or the ricochet of a chough's
cry or the way a voice might move
from *lettuce* to *rocket*
– still a green leaf but peppery tougher

I feel it folded in my pocket
and know it's dull – dull and stained –
that I've written your address on it
and that more much much more is giving me pain
– just touching it is like finding a letter – a love
or a personal letter blowing down the street
so that it feels used dirty torn open
like a cross between a bus ticket's
square of grey print and an unfinished sonnet

# Chagall in Ireland

*for Roy and Aisling Foster*

My childhood *shtetl*
– a mourner slumps down the main street
of this tiny settle-
ment as a halfbrick bursts through my window
while the undented kettle
grows warm on the kosangas stove
like a cat in a basket
– a creaky cricky basket
with a scrap of hairy blanket
that smells of peat
and peat too is hairy
– undaunted the great drayhorse at the forge
turns her luminous eyes
on the nasty fellow
– he's a bad baste –
running down the boreen
where bats will taste flies in the twilight
– asked what'll happen
the march in the next townland
a woman shakes out her apron
oh the night she says
the night will tell the tale
for a moment it's dark and *lumpen*
sort of *Yellow Pages*
but *bather bather* the smith fettles
four metal shoes
for the horse that's glossy and spruce and brown
as ale
and the hill above

– hill with a rath
seems somehow engorged
with what? – I
don't want to say blood
but there is for definite metal
– metal and rust – in the image
and we all know how rust tastes
– tastes like sick
or dried shite
and how it's the colour of the culprit's jacket
– see he's got a stick
in his hand now
– the kettle's plumping
I must turn the gas off
he's skulking in the shadows
waiting for me to come down the path
so he can trip this curlyhaired visitor in the mud
but I'll make him and his stick and his brick
shtick
and like someone signing a letter *with love*
I'll paint him into the far corner

# Bournemouth

*after Verlaine*

The fir trees twist down as far as the shore
– a narrow wood of firs, laurels, pines.
Disguised as a village, the town hides out
in these evergreens – red brick chalets,
then the white villas of the bathing stations.

The inky wood drops down from a heath, a plateau;
comes, goes, scoops out a small valley, then climbs,
    greenblack,
before turning into douce groves that hold the light –
it lays gold on the dark, sleepylooking graveyard
which slopes in steeped stages, laidback, insouciant.

To the left a heavy tower – it has no spire –
squats above the church that's hidden by the trees.
That hard basic tower, the wooden jetty in the distance,
are Anglicanism – brisk, bossy, heartless,
and utterly without hope.

It's the kind of moment I like best
– neither mist nor sunshine, but the sun guessed
from the dissolving mist that melts like a dancer,
as the creamy sky turns pink before it goes.
The air gleams like a pearl, the sea's gold, pure gold.

The protestant tower brangs out a single note,
then two three four, then a batch of eight
pealing out like floating feathers.
Eager, joyous, sad, reproachful,
the metal music's gold, then bronze, then fire.

[118]

Huge but so mild, it coats the narrow wood,
this beautiful sound that travels slowly
over the sea – the sea appears to sing and tremble
the way a road dings and thuds under the boots
of a battalion marching towards the front.

The sound poem's over. But the madder light
drops onto the sea in thick gobbets like sobs
– a cold sunset, another New Year,
a bloodstained town that quivers there in the west
and wears the darkness like a skewed crown.

The evening digs in, icecold, the slatted jetty
vibrates, and the wind in the wood lashes out
and sings as it whips – a cascade of blows
like the hammerbrash of all I've done wrong
– my sins, my betrayals, the people I've hurt.

I'm heartsick, lonely, my soul's a void.
The sea and the winter winds fight it out.
Like a bankrupt actor, I shout out old lines
and turn the night into ambush, catastrophe,
a smell of greasepaint and cheap evil.

Three chimes now, like three notes on a flute.
Three more! three more! it's the Angelus
out of catholic England that says: Peace now,
the Word is made flesh so your sins can be forgiven,
a virgin's womb has quickened, the world is free.

So God speaks through the voice of *His* chapel
– it's halfway up the hill, on the edge of the wood.
Mother Church, Rome, a cry, a gesture,
that calls me back to that one happiness
and makes the rebel bow before the Cross and listen.

The night strokes me, the forgotten jetty
falls silent under the mounting tide.
Luckily there's a straight track marked out
that'll take me home – like a child I hurry
through a wood that's as dark and scary as the Black Forest.

# Sentence Sound

*after Leopardi*

When I was young – about fifteen or so –
five or six pages in a Fontana paperback
on how the ear
is the only true reader
the only true writer
took me into that uncurtained attic
dedicated to the muse
– here poems are often put together
out of fricatives labials and peachy vowels
here prose is stretched or polished
so it doesn't try imitate
the clearness of that blank windowpane
– and because I was taken to this attic
I admired the workbench its wood
all thick and pitted used but sort of raw
like a floor joist or a railway sleeper
– I admired too
the drills gimlets bradawls hammers punches
even though in more than an hour's searching
I couldn't find a single file
– I searched and searched
missing the raspy texture of the thing
until I lifted a long metal tongue
worn quite smooth out of the wastebin
– I licked – no lisped – that smooth file
till it tasted like either hand of a stopped clock

# Drumcree Three

On the day of Drumcree
I took an old pair of red stepladders
out of the garden shed
and set them by a wall
where there's an overgrown vine
– overgrown and unkempt
because the poor plant
faces more or less west
and just as I almost never garden
so its grapes stay small green and bitter
show more dust
than ripe bunches ever do
and always look a bit dead

I climbed the tall
slightly unsteady ladder
and started hackling the vine
all the time careful of a nest
– an abandoned thrush's nest
with three blue eggs
dabbled with olive
– eggs no live
scaldy'd ever crack
they lay there like a line
break that doesn't quite work

as I got stuck into the vine
I could hear on the news
– on the radio news
how the police were hacking a path

through the Garvaghey residents
so that a line
of Orangemen in hundreds
could walk – that is march –
down to the church

I felt tense
tried a phrase from Horace
– it didn't *acris hiems*
make too much sense
and kept working the secateurs
– then we went
to a party in East Hendred
drove home in the dark
like a pair of deserters
and hit the sack with a soft crash

I woke at dawn
and went down to my study
to discover a steep red triangle
still standing on the lawn
outside the window
– standing or parked?
for it's not quite the same thing
and the steps' shade of red
looked more like a dulled madder
in that early light
– light so *frühling* early
it walks
catfooted through curtains

like an idea
– which means that sheer
steep triangle
it might have dropped from the sky
all at once
the way ideas were said to
have fallen on Europe
when Toland was teaching
Irish to Leibniz

or else the ladder
was a Jacob's Ladder
out of a triumphal arch
– DERRY AUGHRIM
the usual NO SURRENDER
a masonic chunk
that had somehow landed
in a garden by the Thames
almost like a set theme
that can't ever
be broken into bits
a kind of dry dream

except the thing looked
more like it had risen out of the earth
or been planted on the grass
like a tiny gantry
or miniature derrick
– the sort you see all over Texas
flexing one arm

as though they were king
of each patch of desert
like a doubly belittled
more recent Ozymandias
– then again it appeared
like a type of cubist
hard metal liberty tree
as I stared at this abstract
rather emptied and formal
opened out object
– object or symbol?
as I looked at this spook
this bloody maddening steel stook
it began in its dumb way
like an opened book
to sing *thing*
*thing thing*
till almost
– and I stress almost
it looked like a dragon's tooth
that had just popped out of the earth
*intil the which it had bin drapped*

# The Wind Dog

*I married a tinker's daughter*
*in the town of Skibbereen*
*but at last one day she galloped away*
*with me only shirt in a paper bag*
*to the shores of Amerikay*

Snug as a foot in a moccasin shoe
– never the boot no never the boot
I lay in Huck's canoe
one still night
and heard men talking
– clean every word they spoke
on the ferry landing
like the Mississippi
was a narra crick
you could hear across
plum as a bell
– one man he reckoned
it was near three o'clock
he hoped daylight wouldn't wait
more'n about a week longer
so there I lay a clockaclay
waitin for the time a'day

logs float down the Mississippi
logs float down the Mississippi
but
but
don't let's start
the whole caper or caber
don't let's ever grow up

*

not to roll out the Logos
– at least at the start
or say in the beginning
was the Word
– not to start with a lingo
with the lingo jingo of beginnings
unsheathed like a sword
stiff and blunt like a phallus
or masonic like a thumb
– not to begin then *arma virumque*
– plush Virgil
but to start with sound
the plumque sound of sense
the bite and the kick of it
– green chilli
kerali
white mooli radish
all crisp and pepper definite
– so my vegetable love did grow
vaster than pumpkins and more slow
for the sound of sense
is what the pretend farmer
– Farmer Frost that is
used call sentence sound
because a sentence he said
was a sound in itself
on which other sounds called words may be strung
which – never not quite iambic though –
is ten syllables that hang together – so
– just so
the way the elephant's child

took seventeen melons
(the green crackly kind)
and said to all his dear families
'Goodbye. I am going to the great
grey-green, greasy Limpopo river,
all set about with fever-trees,
to find out about what the Crocodile has for dinner'
just as Rikki-tikki
– Rikki-tikki-tavi
dates me in a carbon childhood
by this huge swollen river
all along a mill village
– soot bracken and stone
where Mrs Jubb
and Mr Jubb whose leathery right hand
had its thumb missing
– where they lived in a back to back
in a deep warm kitchen with a big kettle
like a pet
lived by the music of that bulgy river
that bulgy bulgy river
wider and deeper and slopping at the bank
ever and always ever and always
all those torn waters turning dark
in maybe October
as though the world itself had become bigger and wilder
than the world itself could ever be
because world is suddener than we fancy it
big with itself
*gonflé*

now I know the source
– the elephant child
of the tram that tatty doubledecker
that stood out from the others
– blue and icecream white
or fire engine red they were
– but the tatty one
*that* was the fever tram and it slid
sinister along the main
the dangerous main road
at the bottom of Wensley Drive
in Leeds Yorkshire
in Leeds *Yorkshire*
– which is a change of sound accent place
so let me trawl and list
a couple or three sounds in my archive
– not the images
not the pictures
there must – because the ear
the ear is the only true reader –
there must be nothing seen or sighted
no moral message neither
no imperative
because out of the ocean of all sound
one little drop
two little drop
three little drop
shall come forth and fall back
as Rikki-tikki
that other the grey-green

greasy Limpopo river
the green crackly melons
and the snake eggs
– eggs with a skin not a shell
that're buried in a melon bed
or a crack in a mud wall
where Rikki-tikki
is snacking
on the tops of the eggs
– this is like buried bakelite
the headphones on my crystal set
– or the set my strikebreaking uncle
built back in the 20s
in the attic of 7 Deramore Drive
he set the aerial on a telegraph pole
in the garden of a house called Invergowrie
a house off the Malone Road
with tartan curtains – Robertson tartan –
and a lectric bell under the diningroom carpet
to call the maid
who'd left way back as surely as Louis MacNeice
alias Louis Malone had left
the city on the lough
and then had shuffled off this wiry copper coil
long before the city hit the news again

but it's not the dring of that bell
I'd press so my granny'd think
it was the front door
it's a woman – a jum –

in an untidy room
its greasy cushions hookah
a few sweetmeats
– green pistachio
on a shiny tin plate
at the edge of a brass tray
the huge and shapeless woman
clad in greenish gauzes
and decked
brow nose ear neck wrist arm waist and ankle
with heavy native jewellery
when she turned
it was like the clashing of copper pots
– even she banged a bangle against the tray
when she lifted it to offer me
one of those green sweetmeats
a vein of the gospel proffer the grub the prog
– you know the cargo cult line
that dirty British coaster
its cheap tin trays
cheap tin trays
that's the music speaks me
sings me
makes me
cheeps me
but it's also the cheapo rings on a curtain pole
the way they clishclash too
– something greasy there
greasy or oily
a mixture of brass and unction

like a skitter of listless syllables
that makes me ask
what am I hearing?
what am I knowing?
as the woman – the jum –
in baggy pants
plumps the cushions back into shape
– again the slickslock of her bangles
those silk cushions
the sigh of Hindi being spoken
spoken and then sung
because it's all surface like Matisse
odalisque Matisse
and I'm a child again
a child that reads and hears
but doesn't understand
– who neither comprehends
this nor that
nor the silk sash my father never wore
before the heavens
before the silksack clouds were filled
with the clashing of swords
before I asked Brian Fearon
how much his bottle of orange
– his *bottulornj* cost?
and he said *thhee dee*

then showed me a little brass
little brass hexagonal
thrupenny bit

in the palm of his catholic hand
so I heard *thhee*
for the very first time
on the half between North
and South Parade
before ever I heard it come back in song
– *thhee black lumps*
*outa her wee shap*
– *candy apples hard green pears*
*kanversation lazengers*
which is all beginning
all beginning still
yet if I wanted to put a date
when this naked shivering self
began to puzzle at print sound
spokensound
the wind in the reeds
or a cry in the street
I'd choose that room for a start
the bangles
the curtain rings
– it's my baby tuckoo
tuckoo tuckoo it is
not the tundish
this is echt British
except that's always fake somehow
it's machinery means of production
not a spring well
– the well of Anglish
or the well of Oirish undefiled

for this isn't when
but where it happened
where ice burned
and was but the more ice
and salted was my food and my repose
salted and sobered too by the bird's call
the golden bird who perched
on his golden bough
to sing that ancient salt
is best packing
that all that is mortal of great Plato there
is stuck like chewed gum
in Tess's hair
which happened – as it had to –
before ever I seen those tinned kippers
packed into boxes
on the quayside
in Cullercoats or Whitley Bay
and my great aunt
takes the penny ferry over the Tyne
and my English not my Scots granny
calls me *hinny*
and it feels
– that houyhnhnm whinny
of the northeast coast
almost like love and belonging
so I ask myself
why does Elaine Tweedie
say *tarr* not *tar?*
why do I glance down

at her skirt – yellanblack tartan
skirt – when she says it?
what is it almost touching me
like skin warm skin?
I mean we live in two streets
off the same road
– the Ormeau Road
why should we say it different?
and why does my mother say *modren*
not *modern*?
a modrun nuvel not a modern novel
a *fa*natic not a fanatic
which is a way of saying
this is my mother tongue
the gold torc
second time out
for out of Ireland have we sort of come
to find in a book called *The Hamely Tongue*
that the word jum
means a 'large, unreliable trouble-giving car'
as well – it's the dipstick talking –
as 'a large, lazy and probably none too clean woman'
so did that word – the word *jum* –
bob over the sheugh to Broagh
to the riverbroo
the mudshelf of the bank?
or is it Ulstermade?
would you puzzle me that one?
puzzle me proper
while I'm out after mackerel

in an open boat
– blue blue sky
after a skift of rain
the wet wondrous sky
stretched tight like a bubble

– hey Tammie Jack says
d'you see thon wind dog?
look yonder
– what's a wind dog captain?
– ack a wee broken bitta rainbow
tha's a wind dog

we were neither off Coney Island
nor floating down Cypress
Avenoo
– we were out
in the Gweebarra Bay
so I say to myself *Gweebarra*
and drive westward
leaving the picky saltminers
of Carrickfergus behind
me and that lover
of women and Donegal
– 'ack Louis poor Louis!'
was all Hammond's aunt the bishop's
housekeeper could say at the end
it was too looey late to tape her
she was too far gone
what with age and with drink

hardly a mile to go
before she shleeps
hardly a mile to go
before she shleeps
– there used be such crack in that kitchen
her and the maid
always laughing and yarning the pair of them
and wee Louis in the room above
hearing the brangle of talk
rising through the floorboards

o chitterin chatterin platinum licht
the bow shall be in the clouds
and I will look upon it
to remember the everlasting testament
between God and all that liveth upon earth
whatsoever flesh or faith it be
– they may have turned Tyndale into tinder
but the bow he wrought lives high
in this wet blue sky

hardly a mile to go
through the deep deep snow
as I follow another poet's
long shivering shadow
over the crumping snow
– not the journey out of Essex
nor the journey – yet –
out of Egypt
its chisel chipping stone

this is us walking snow
– its widewhite horizon dazzle
the soft quoof
and near crump of it
under our boots
their leather thin and soft
as moccasins
our feet cauld
– *crump crump crump* we go
like break of day in the trenches
as our breath spoofs
in the frore air
soundlessly collateral
and incompatible

how cauld it is
out on air
for the very first time
but not as gross and crass
as the first studio in Belfast
its acoustic deadness
– every wall and bit of furniture muffled
not a shred of echo –
where a cheery *good day*
or – it's Tyrone Guthrie talking –
a ringing roundelay
fell with a dull thud
into a sterilized blank
so two comedians' backchat
it sounded like one mute

telling dirty stories
to another mute in an undertaker's parlour
– so there was none
– it's almost a daft term
like the name of a flower
– none of that 'recorded ambience'
which means the putting back
of silence between sounds
so in the undertaker's studio
there was none
of the living hum of silence
because silence
isn't the absolute absence of sound
– that's death
the undertaker's parlour
silence is the barm the rise the yeast
– so never let those horny feet protood
just parle parle parle
go eat
banana nut ice cream
in a parlour off Ormeau Avenoo
– it's cauld but
like the battlements
on Elsinore
a nipping and an eager air
– *eager* I suppose as in *aigre*
meaning *vinegary bitter acid*
meaning *keen sharp*
like the blade of a knife
no a knifeblade

– put a spondee boy
place a the anapæst!
this is exposure
the here and the now
where we look round the muddy compound
– walls made of tin
or stone or brick
and soggy with sound
wet sound
where we feel
like sick to death almost
a generation
that has come so far
in darkness and in pain
that has heard the sound
– behold we have no continuing city
of gunfire
down streets and over fields
and rooftops
at the Giant's Ring
Shipquay Street
Divis
the Ormeau and a thousand other
roads and streets and fields
round after round after round
– that has heard the sound
of culvert bomb upon culvert bomb
that plump and heavy sound
that tells us
– master of the still stars

never such innocence again
as it dumps and bumps and crumps
over the snow
near Swordy Well
there's a frozen lane between stone walls
– high stone walls
listen
*our nailed boots wi clenching tread rebound*
*& dithering echo starts and mocks the clamping sound*
– all the way
from the acoustic deadness of that studio in Linenhall Street
to the poet who died
in the same asylum as Lucia Joyce
– *Yet what I am none cares or knows*
*My friends forsake me like a memory lost*
*I am the selfconsumer of my woes*
– all the way
to a brook in Northamptonshire
*Were as one steps its oaken plank*
*The hollow frozen sounding noise*
*From flags & sedge beside the bank*
*The wild ducks brooding peace destroys*

walking the plank
we turn the bridge into a thunderbox
– blocks of dead sound
drop *bock bock bock*
into the air
as though something formal and dreadful
is both happening and about to happen

on this wooden platform
– sound is always ahead of itself
– at least sound that has an echo
and a living skin of air
ambient air
around it
so sound is both Being and Becoming
like that river that bulgy river
where I walked with Mrs Jubb
one maybe October evening
in the third or fourth year
of this
my life

# Le Crapaud

*after Corbière*

An airless night a sort of song
– moon a metal plaque
its tattery shadows inky green
. . . buried alive under those laurel roots
the song's a slimy echo pulsing pulsing
– he shuts up – look he's down by the drain
– a toad! his pursy skin pubbles
but I'm guarding him with my own skin
– look at him – a wingless poet bald as a coot
a mud nightingale a singing turd
. . . he starts his song again *yuk yuk yuk*
why'm I disgusted? see the light in his eyes
no – he flubs under some mooncold rubble

\*

night night – fat Mr Turd he's me

# Oxford

This morning I pass a big clump of purple buddleia
by the river and catch their honeyed scent
and notice again how they're shaped like *kulfi*
– like Indian icecream
then as I walk towards the Bodleian
there's this old man finishing a yellow dream –
like enormous watercolour of the Radcliffe
Camera – perhaps he's a nephew
of Charles Ryder? with that precious nostalgia
which might be all this cavalier place is meant
to mean though take that word *camera*
and you'll find it means *room* in Latin
just as the word *kamra* in Punjabi
also means *room*
so that from the Land of the Five Rivers
to Ancient Rome
to this three hundred year and more dome
is as short and sweet as a piece of *burfi*

# The Emigration of the Poets

*after Brecht*

Homer belonged nowhere
and Dante he'd to leave home
as for Tu Fu and Li Po
they did a flit through the smoke
– 30 million were no
more in those civil wars
while the high courts
tried stuff Euripides under the floor
and even Shakespeare got a gagging order
as he lay dying in Stratford
– Villon who wrote 'Les Pendus'
had visits from the Muse
and from the Beast
– i.e. the police
though at least Lucretius
was nicknamed *Le bien aimé*
and slipped away from *Heim*
just like Heine
– now watch me here Bertolt Brecht
I'm a pike
shtuck in this Danish thatch

*from* THE INVASION HANDBOOK

# Prologue

Koba is in a country
no a wilderness province
the size of Scotland
– nine months of ice and snow
they live in caves where his fellow
exiles fear the hard glints
in his eyes his yellow
smoky eyes that hex his comrades
and will them toward the shades
summer's hot – they move to shacks and tents
– the tents sailcloth the shacks tarred
always aloof and solitary
he imagines becoming the metal Shah
the steel Tsar I mean
of all the Russias
gravedigger hangman knotting his rope
the hardest of hard cases
he will one day forge – yes *forge*
a new a rigid Europe
but for this stretch he's on the far mar-
gins of a wrinkled no not a withered state
that's broken at the head and hips
alone on the taiga
– a clanging bird somewhere –
he places a juniper berry on his lips
sucks then rolls it on his tongue
a tiny bit of gunge
it tastes quite deliciously bitter
now with one
one as yet undreaded hand

he scratches his head for a long long
time like a patient tiger
though in his best and worst dreams
this drunken shoemaker's son
is Caesar inside a nutmeg or an almond
the king of infinite space
with the power to bring the world to an end
though all these four long years
he knows he has pitched his tent
upon a grain of sand

# Clemenceau

'faut commencer avec Clemenceau
in no way clement
and forbidding like a pot palm
– sterile and fruitless
his pitted cheeks scurfbark
in a room dry like a hotpress
where they tried le Conseil des Quatres
to live the dead
to grind peace into its opposite
as though they'd met in a stranded diningcar
inside the Hall of Mirrors
to sing a psalm –
when Israel went into Egypt
there was heard the plockplock of horsehooves
a toltering bustle clipped scatter
like sabots clocking the cobbles
in some Rhineland town
black as the cavern null and void
of the Empire fireplace
in that hot dry room
with its marble its leafy mirror
the glass dome over a snowy owl
un hibou blanc comme une colombe
brooding on a black abyss
or as snow falling softly
so very very softly
like leaves millions of leaves
reeling down on all those
who would say if they could
*I am not yet born*

while out of the night and the snow
rises the hunting sovereign dove
as these four men the cloud compellers
weigh Germany's guilt like gold or diamonds
or a tiny heap of dust
in the shivering trivial
skittery unforgiving balance

no one knows that I Georges Clemenceau
– I the Tiger
no one knows I made war
with 40 grammes of sugar in my blood
senem annis animo juvenum
– the Latin orator in the Sheldonian
made me Christ the Tiger
in the juvescence – wrong springy word –
of the year
the cruel time of the year
my father a Jacobin
who hung a portrait of Robespierre
a portrait of St Just
in our house in the Vendée
– marsh plain bocage
I have been faithful to our good earth
to Dreyfus
and have been ever and always an enemy
to the guillotine
though Rodin's bust it makes me
a Mongolian general
my apartment is brimful

of Manets and Monets
– long before I wrote
my book – heart of light – on *Les Nymphéas*
Monet gave me *Le Bloc*
the prophet's mountain top
for it was given this prophet to more than know
that the Germans are a peuple servile
that needs force
to support an argument
– Napoleon before he died
said that nothing fixed
nothing permanent
can be founded on force
me I'm not so sure
a hundred years for you Americans
is a very long time
for us it's not much
I've known men who saw Napoleon
with their own eyes
America is faraway
protected by the Ocean
England couldn't be reached
by Napoleon himself
you are both of you safe
we are not

# The Skeleton

*after Verlaine*

Two pachles both stocious are lurching back
over a battlefield – they're doubles of our old friend
the miles gloriosus and they look bulky like sacks
so maybe they're Hessians who like Jack Falstaff
are – mortal men sir – full of sack
and sorry the war has staggered to an end
but then they see this gnawed daft
– nit of a translator says *deboned* – skeleton
lying there among the puddles and shellholes
the mud the debris the bust or abandoned weapons
– like a trapdoor its mouth gapes open
as it lies there static a bleached symbol of ending
then Captain Bones cranks up and addresses our two
    squaddies
– more to come – tell the ranks – more great more
    dulce days!

# August 39

In a house called Invergowrie
– Scotch baronial South Belfast
prosperous and Calvinist
she dreams an open boat
packed with a series
of starved figures
their ribcages bare as laths
– a hint somewhere in the story
(all dreams must tell a story)
that this has to do
with statistics or maths
– the sun is visible and hot
as an almost breeze makes ziggers
on the bluesmooth
surface of the ocean
that's as tight and sinister
as the phrase she'll bring back
from this involuntary journey
– *a dream and a fear*
for now she knows
that many miles from dry land
these ancient mariners
are entering their last sleep
they differ
from the corpse she saw last month
on the dissecting table
the corpse two students dressed
in an old overcoat
and played games with
as if it were a guy

ready for the bonfire
or as if it was a man full
of drink – but as the sea
is also known as the drink
there may be more to this than we think

not an oar but a gaff
– useless thing – leans in one rowlock
and that large hook
it spells out
all that she can see before her
and around and inside her
– a type of horror she hasn't met
with ever that's lodged in her now
like a message from father stamped
on her young mind
that six seven years later
she'll learn to understand
until years beyond
those newsreels of the camps
she hands her dream on
to her eldest son
who wonders if mere dreams
can weigh in the record
or for that matter can poems?

# Churchill

*10/5/40*

Telegrams ribbed cardboard boxes of telegrams
from dawn on they spat and kicked
– klotzen nicht kleckern
into the Admiralty the War
and the Foreign Office
– the Germans had struck
their long awaited blow
now the whole huge movement
of that army I had warned against
all my parched years in the wilderness
was pushing and crushing
all that stood in its path

they said Winston you must preserve
a complete why an absolute
a jammy silence
– if you speak first
then you're lost
– at eleven that morning
I was again summoned to Downing Street
by the prime minister
and there once again
I found Halifax had preceded me
like a secondguesser
or an ample
familiar ghost
robed in ermine
– or was it Chamberlain's ghost
his ghost to be

I saw in the far corner
of that drawingroom chill and fixed
like a stage set?
– it was a trap
this arranged meeting
between a dying man
a former viceroy
and myself
– the powers in the land
they all wanted Lord
Safe Pair of Hands Halifax
– the King Chamberlain Attlee
all behind him while I
was a reckless adventurer
strapped by the Dardanelles
the Duke of Windsor
and Norway
– how could I break their will?
this was a trap for a Trappist
unless – ho you've guessed it –
I kept my corny trap shut
a silent invisible man
or abstract ghost
though I felt more like a Michelin man
snug in my blubber
of tubby silence
– then Chamberlain spoke
I said nothing twice
like a monk trying to hear
the sound of one hand clapping

I underlined nothing with silence
I dotted the *i* in *nothing*
with silence then gazed
into the almost ostentatious
rubber tyre of its *o*
oh no
this was a silence longer
than the two minutes we observe
on Armistice Day
a moment of more than quiet
but crowded with all those shades
standing proud above their broken bodies
out of time and in time too
a moment that first chilled
to absolute zero
then built to the knowledge
that the whole of my life
had brought me like Aeneas
to this one glimpse of the Latian shore
– Behold the Lord the Lord of hosts
shall lop the bough with terror
and the high one of stature shall be hewed down
and the haughty shall be humbled
– was I the prophet
or did the prophet speak against me?
it was then I felt
– felt unbearable on my shoulders
the burden of the desert
the burden of the desert of the sea
and Babylon fallen fallen

but still I wrapped myself
in the mummy cloth of my silence
while the silence in the room
held like a high dam
– then Halifax spoke
– no dam now a bridge
over a clear bubbling stream
– as a peer
I am of course out of the House of Commons
upon whose confidence the life
of each and every government depends
– I cannot therefore
be prime minister
– at six I went to the Palace
and at three that morning
the prophet vindicated
sank gratefully into his bed

# Boca do Inferno

A state secret I want to unlock
is Hitler's wedding present to the Duke
and Duchess of Windsor – a little gold box
that may by some fluke
have survived in a locked archive
where we might read the inscription
that looks forward to his restoration
zu seinem rechtmäßigen Thron
– his rightful throne
but we may never know why Rudolf Hess
flew all the way to Lisbon
– never know exactly but we can guess
that Victor/Hess told Willi/Duke
of the plan to fly him to Germany
where as a spy he would secretly
be awarded the Iron Cross
– yes the Iron Cross First Class
which would one day soon be welded to his crown

*from* THE ROAD TO INVER

# The Island in the North Sea

*Rilke*

Each farm squats inside a circular dam
like a fort a bawn a crater on the moon
bashed by storms each garden looks the same
and has it rough like an unloved orphan

who counts the bodies of drowned fishermen and grieves
as the islanders they keep indoors and stare
at crooked mirrors that show nicknames fancy things
among the delph that stacks each dresser

after tea some youth might take a dander
and rasp a tune on his harmonica
– its tacky girning he picked it up

in a foreign port some dockside bar
– then a sheep scumbles up a dyke a
gross hirpling dopey ominouslooking sheep

# The Albatross

*Baudelaire*

Marilyn and the cassowary bird
– its head's protected by a bony helmet or casque –
they both know what the other bird's about
– idle gliding comrade of endless
voyages over tradescarred seas
where mariners counting the sea's clock
skrimshander whalebone or tempt him onto the deck
where with two left feet he paddles
on the dry boards – boards as stiff
as the ship's biscuit they chuck
at him – as well try swallow grey coke
or clinker – now some tar smoking a clay pipe takes
it and gives his long bony beak
– his glossy beak – a hard poke
another splays his feet out and hops
with as much grace as a sack
of old potatoes caked in mud
then laughs at the poor craychur he's mocking
– yes we know that the poet any star like Marilyn
and the cassowary too resemble the albatross
– whole crowds rough as those jack
tars squatting on sunscrubbed boards yak
away at them all – then with gossip and innuendo
– how they roll their tongues on the name *Monroe* –
they lay each in turn on their back
and rip out their guts

# Belongings

*Khazendar*

Who entered my room when I was out
and moved the vase on the mantelpiece just a tad?
who skewed that print – a Crusader – on the far wall?
and those pages loose on my desk
they're a shade dishevelled aren't they?

of course someone's read them
and my pillow's never been dented this way
– not by any lovely head
that stray shirt I'd never leave on the floor
– some shit's dropped it

so who came into my room? who?
and who'll put the vase back exactly
as it was? who'll
straighten the mailed knight in his corner?
and who'll restore to my shirt and pillow
their full rights as citizens
of my single room?

# To a Political Poet

*Heine*

Your baggy lyrics,
they're like a cushion
stuffed with smooth grudges
and hairy heroes.

'Me Mam's Cremation',
'Me Rotten Grammar School',
'Ode to the Toffee-Nosed Gits
Who Mocked My Accent'.

Now your whinges
get taught in class
and the kids feel righteous –
righteous but cosy.

# The Briar

*Baudelaire*

An author owns me – I'm his pipe
my complexion it's coalblack – collied – like that
of a slavegirl he's rescued but I'm glad to let
him believe this as with one feely finger he tamps in the shag

when he's really sad I'm like a thatched
cabin with smoke rising from its chimney
– his missus is cooking a heavy supper
for the ploughman slumped on the settle

I tie up his soul and stroke it softly
in the silky blue net
that curls up from my hot lips

the rings I make are so so balmy
they soothe his heart and spirit
then the poor man doesn't he start to feel happy?

*from* LOVE'S BONFIRE

# A Day with Two Anniversaries

Our aim – no mine –
was to slash the badger
(that's such bad language)
but we hit a real one
on the road to Drumquin
– too late
I saw his eyes greeny red
in the headlights
(couldn't – didn't – stop)
as the heavy *chump* confirmed
Drumquin's maybe dodgy name
but the hill the beat the walk
always inside it
– inside the drum the hill –
they promised more
– more of the same –
as – staying B&B
we sat in Harkin's Bar
looking at those two humped bookends
with the local news
going on above their heads
while they talked and drank
– one phrase I caught from that report
was *body parts*
another *cap badge*
– later we'd retire
to a lumpy bed in a room across the yard
a bed that smelt of old newspapers
– nothing was said
in that oh that dread room

a few miles from what had been your home
then like a fell arrest
I put one hand on your shoulder
but we'd no desire
no not in that damp
damp as well as dodgy bed

# A Noticed Thing

The windsock by the airfield
it's hanging flaccid this evening
– hanging flaccid on its white pole
by the perimeter
I happen on it this hot humid Friday
like the way you find *a symbol*
in a poem or a novel
– something that's over- or predetermined
– something like that
or like this too obvious giant condom
with the teat snipped off
which takes us back to the static
empty windsock drained of its usual orange colour
– your name is on me it says
on me like a bullet
I can tell you're shocked
well just a tad you are
at being spoken to by a flat
– you called me flaccid –
by a flat windsock
– let me remind you
I was your image at one time
for the whole world
for everything-that-is-the-case
plus the wind rushing through it
or gulshing through it if you like
but perhaps you've moved on?
As you can see I'm all used up
like some friend you've left behind
– the world though is not conclusion
stuff that in your sock and ate it

# Elm Tree Avenue

We set up home
in a Victorian semi
in what only with hindsight
was a rather dull suburb
where we were so happy
painting walls and scrubbing floors
putting up curtains and going to auctions
at 9 every Saturday
in the grim cattlemarket.
At the back of the house
there was a small garden
the size of a diningtable
a low hedge and a gate
that led into a playingfield
where children would play
and where I once found a tortoise
our neighbours the Foxes
had lost a year back.
Beyond it was a tennis court
where one summer's evening
during the Queen's Silver Jubilee
I watched the players
suddenly drop their racquets
and stand firmly to attention
as the National Anthem
wafted from the bandstand
by the river beyond the houses.
This is another country I thought
with different manners and customs.
The English I came to see

have very good manners
– Etonians have the best –
but the Irish I've learnt
have even better manners.
Old enemies can break bread together
and shout and laugh at each other
but part the best of new friends.
This never works at an English suppertable
maybe because the English
are rather more honest
– with them what you see is what you get
– it's that plain and simple

# Kissing Ms Khosa

Tip is touch
– as in tiptoe
or – better – on tiptoe
which is a bit like being unsteady in a church
or tin bible hall or gudwara
or it's like walking – no teetering – on stilts
or trying to talk under your breath
in a less than stealthy whisper
and being also unready
like a foal or a lamb that's just been shoved from the womb
like shit from a shovel
– a little lickspittle – yella – wobbling
on its pins in the mud wary
and doubly unsteady
as it trembles and touches the wet earth
like broken like chittering light
– yes a wee wind dog
or like that moment when the tips of our tongues first touched
which again was like walking on tiptoe
– daring but with qualms –
inside a packed or an empty church
– or tin hut I mean hall or gudwara –
wary we might trip over even though your
breasts and nipples were as yet untouched
by my fingers and palms or my lips either

so tip is beginning?
– no just the start

# Love's Bonfire

One dark October evening
at the almost innocent age
of twenty-one
my love and I were walking in secret along a rough track
by the High School in Fivemiletown.
An army jeep passed down the road
(it was near the start of the Troubles).
We'd just started out
and had to be careful
not in the usual way
(that was a long way off)
but for fear of her extended family
– it was a time – it still is
of honour killings.
So we walked slowly in darkness
intent but tremulous
at this brave new so-tender thing between us
soft and tiny as a lark's egg.
We walked not quite a couple
always careful not to hold hands
(I knew that I must never
try to snatch a kiss).
So we walked slowly in the darkness
like a couple who didn't know where they were going.
By the side of the path we found
what looked like a dead bonfire.
We stared at it for a bit and then you took a stick
and began to stir
the dead embers.
From under the soft white ash

the red embers started
and as you raked and raked them
all the soft ash fell away
till they glowed and began to flame
on top of their bed of defeated ash.
So the bonfire started again and came warmly alive
as a whole big bed
of silent red embers.
I saw then I recall
that we were quite different people
– you were active
didn't want the arranged marriage
and believed we had a future
while I feared that it – the marriage
would happen for definite
and saw your mother weeping your father mad angry
the tough cousins massing
you saying no this can never be Tom
and me saying wanly
Giti I love you so dearly
and I will for always
but I see you can't bring shame
down on your family your tribe.
I had no trust we would ever
though we'd declared our love
in anguish for each other
– that we'd ever be together
for ever and ever
as the books used to say.
Forty years on

in a deep dark time
with a permanent pain always in my head
I see where that pain began.
I think if I asked you
could you call that moment back
– a moment we've never spoken of
all these long years
you'd say only
veteris vestigia flammae
– though I pray that you wouldn't.

# Putting the Pan On

Daithe was a headbanger
and a sort of poet
– an Ulster protestant a Unionist
so a rare kind of bird.

He lived in a soggy cottage
with Concepta in Wiltshire
(she wasn't his wife
– he'd left her years back).

We spent a night with them
drinking talking and laughing
'Here I am' said Daithe
'banging about like a bee in a tin

trying to get the pan on.'
About 10 that night
Daithe finally got the pan on
– he dropped a lump of cod

into the lardy frying pan
but didn't know that he should've
dusted it with flour
or coated it in egg and breadcrumbs.

We ate the sad pallid cod
and drank more red wine
then left in the morning
laughing all the way

through the deep green Wye Valley
at Daithe and Concepta
a happy couple
who would quarrel and make up

ten times a day.
Then last thing in our hotel
I remember you smiling as you peeled
silver foil from a bar of black chocolate

then pressing a square on my tongue
before we made love still laughing
at Daithe the bee in the tin
always about to put the pan on.

# Saggy

Rembrandt's drawing of an elephant
is yes a drawing of that mild
displaced creature a real elephant
so loose and baggy you'd never think
it belonged ever to the wild
but if you blink
you'll see it's an almost child-
like portrait of the artist
his pouchy tragic vigilant
and softened face waiting for the fist

# Floragrande

Way way back – two centuries or more –
a couple of seeds made a journey
by road and by ocean from India
they were stuck in a hemp bag
hemp or hessian was it?
or maybe a carpet bag
on the Grand Trunk Road?
and those seeds changed themselves
into a great magnolia
– green waxy magnificent –
once the gardener had dibbed them
into the warm earth on the shores
the shores of Lake Como
so the years went by and those seeds
grew into something enormous
– blossoms like tulips –
a great big airy cage
somewhere between a bush and a tree
a tree or a huge bucket
plonked upside down on a beach
if you see what I mean
– c'était Pierre Magnol
qui a donné le nom
and that's the honest truth
according to Tom